Good Moaning France!

Officer Crabtree's Fronch Phrose Berk

ISBN 978-1-909976-59-7 (Paperback)
ISBN 978-1-910979-69-3 (Epub ebook)
ISBN 978-1-910979-70-9 (Adobe ebook)

Copyright © 2018 This work is the copyright of Arthur Bostrom. All intellectual property and associated rights are hereby asserted and reserved by the author in full compliance with UK, European and international law. No part of this book may be copied, reproduced, stored in any retrieval system or transmitted in any form or by any means, including in hard copy or via the internet, without the prior written permission of the publishers to whom all such rights have been assigned worldwide.

Cover design © 2018 Waterside Press.

Cover and other illustrations by John Cooper.

Printed by CPI, Chippenham, UK.

Main UK distributor: Gardners Books, 1 Whittle Drive, Eastbourne, East Sussex, BN23 6QH. Tel: +44 (0)1323 521777; sales@gardners.com; www.gardners.com

North American distribution: Ingram Book Company, One Ingram Blvd, La Vergne, TN 37086, USA. Tel: (+1) 615 793 5000; inquiry@ingramcontent.com

A catalogue record can be obtained from the British Library.

e-book: *Good Moaning France! Officer Crabtree's Fronch Phrase Berk* is available as an ebook and also to subscribers of Ebrary, Ebsco, Myilibrary and Dawsonera.

Published 2018 by:
Waterside Press Ltd
Hook, Hampshire, United Kingdom.
Telephone +44(0)1256 882250
Online catalogue WatersidePress.co.uk
Email enquiries@watersidepress.co.uk

Good Moaning France!

Officer Crabtree's Fronch Phrose Berk

Arthur Bostrom

With a Foreword by Rick Wakeman

Illustrations by John Cooper

WATERSIDE PRESS

Contents

About the author *x*
About the artist *x*
Reviews *xi*
Foreword *xiii*
The author of the Foreword *xiv*

Acknowledgements *xv*
Dedication *xvii*
Disclaimer *xix*
List of Illustrations *xx*
Ask Crabtree *xx*

Introduction _____ 21

1. **Out and About** _____ 25

    A Poloceman's Newt Berk (1) 28
    Numbers 28

2. **Wartime Phrases** _____ 31

    A Poloceman's Newt Berk (2) 34
    Victory Phrases 34

3. **French Language Rules** _____ 37
    School Words.. 38

4. **My Everyday Practice** _____ 39
    My Daily Routine 40

5. **Everyday Words and Phrases** _____ 41
    Objects... 41
    Newspapers 42
    Everyday Conversational Words.............. 43
    Food and Beverage 44
    In the Home... 47

🔁 *A Poloceman's Newt Berk (3)*		49
	Christmas Words	50
6. **Going on Holiday to France**		51
	Essentials	51
	At the Airport or Ferry	52
	Clothes for Men	55
	Clothes for Women	55
	Everything Else	56
	On the Beach	56
	Helpful Phrases for a Beach Holiday	57
	Packing for a Walking Holiday	59
	Sightseeing	62
	Camping and Caravanning Holidays	62
🔁 *A Poloceman's Newt Berk (4)*		66
	Everyday Words	66
	Meeting a Policeman	69
	French Words Concerning Crime	70
7. **All About Banking**		73
8. **Shopping**		75
	Useful Words for Clothes Shopping	76
	Useful Phrases When Food Shopping	77
	Useful Words When Food Shopping	78
🔁 *A Poloceman's Newt Berk (5)*		80
	Highway Code	80
	Other Words	80

9. Living and Working in France ___ 83

Office Words 83

Everyday Office Phrases 87

A Poloceman's Newt Berk (6) 89

Rescue Words 90

10. Music ___ 91

Types of Music 91

Classical Composers 92

Popular Musicians of the 60s, 70s and 80s 93

Modern Pop Stars 94

Music for a 'Romantic Mood' 95

A Poloceman's Newt Berk (7) 97

Crime Words 98

11. Proverbs ___ 99

A Poloceman's Newt Berk (8) 103

Bonfire Words 104

12. Books ___ 107

Further Reading *109*

Undex *110*

By kind permission

Based on the original character created by David Croft and Jeremy Lloyd

Arthur Bostrom

About the author

Arthur Bostrom appeared as Officer Crabtree in eight series of the BBC TV series *'Allo 'Allo!* (still repeated in the UK and sold to over 80 countries worldwide). He also appeared in the stage version of the show, which ran for five seasons in London's West End as well as tours of the UK, New Zealand and Australia. Arthur was born in Rugby and later graduated in Geography from the University of Durham. An actor for forty years, he has appeared in many theatre, TV and radio productions. He is also a voice-over artist, life coach and Fellow of the Royal Geographical Society.

About the artist

John Cooper is an illustrator and stand-up comedian based in Manchester. Creating the original comic caricatures of officer Crabtree with Arthur Bostrom adds to his already diverse artwork portfolio which includes TV adverts, music festivals and comic books. You can view his work at johncooper.org.uk

'Listen very carefully, you will read this more than once. I loaved it'.
Les Dennis

'I've not laughed at anything like I've laughed at Crabtree ever in my life, this book is "very good nose"'.
Justin Moorhouse

'Buck your fairy trip to Fronce now and take Crabtree's guide with you. A must-read. Hilarious'.
Su Pollard

'Гордея се, че "родих" Полицай Крабтрий на български. Никога не съм предполагала, че хиляди българи ще започнат да се поздравяват с "Добрютро", благодарение на моя превод! Златна Костова, преводач на Ало! Ало! в България'.
Zlatna Kostova, translator of 'Allo 'Allo! for Bulgaria*

'Met de broer van Crabtree in mijn film ontzettend veel lol gehad tijdens de opnames in Nederland. Jammer dat het alweer een tijd terug is. Met plezier heb ik dit boek gelezen en kan het iedereen aanraden'.
Martijn van Nellestijn, Film Director and Producer from The Netherlands†

'DO NOT BUY ZIS BOOK!!! IF YOU DO, YOU VILL BE SHOT!!!'
Helga

---

* 'I am very proud to have "given birth" to Officer Crabtree in Bulgarian. I never expected thousands of Bulgarians to start greeting each other with "Good Moaning", thanks for this!'

† 'We had a lot of fun with the brother of Crabtree in my film during shooting in The Netherlands. Too bad it's been a while back. I read this book with pleasure and can recommend it to everyone'.

Foreword

As an avid lover of all things David Croft, when 'Allo 'Allo! first hit our television screens in 1982, it had myself and huge audiences hooked for many reasons.

As well as being hysterically funny, men of all ages drooled over Vicki Michelle and dreamt of being a German officer in order to experience for themselves the lure of the wet celery whilst wearing a flying helmet.

As with all David Croft's work, the characters were all beautifully crafted by him (and here his co-writer Jeremy Lloyd) and by the second series were familiar to us all and then, just when we thought that any more characters couldn't be introduced, in the middle of the second series, 'The Policeman Cometh' hit our screens with a genius line as Officer Crabtree burst through the door of *Café Rene* and announced to the gathered throng the immortal words … 'Good Moaning'.

I remember falling off my chair. It was hysterical and from that moment on Officer Crabtree was in the hearts of the nation. I have lost count of the number of times he was 'just pissing by the café' and I often wondered how he would have said 'Forty Winks'. (I did ask David once and he said 'Wouldn't have got past the censors Rick').

I love books about sit-coms. I really love it when they are written by an involved and greatly loved actor. I am sure Arthur 'can only write this once', so make sure you read it 'very carefully'.

As an afterthought I do think there perhaps should be an additional book though ... *Officer Crabtree's Guide to Speaking Colloquial French* or perhaps *Farty Woos to Spook to Frigs*.

Rick Wakeman
September 2018

The author of the Foreword

Music legend Rick Wakeman is an English keyboard player, songwriter, presenter and author best known for his many albums released since the 1970s and as a member of the rock band Yes.

Acknowledgements

So many people have helped me and encouraged me to both write and finish this book. I list them here with love and gratitude.

Thank you to Kim Hartman, Su Pollard, Les Dennis, Justin Moorhouse, Zlatna Kostova and Martijn Van Nellestijn for contributing your strap lines.

Thank you to Rick Wakeman for the Foreword.

Thank you to Penny Croft, Lizzie Lloyd, Tim Hancock and Laura Rourke for your support.

Thank you to these fuse lighters and encouragers who gave me early and continued support: Eleanor Ford, Cliff Ford, Liam McCormick, Pat Lomax, Brainne Edge, Rob Hudson, Sian Prime, Simon Jermy, Liz Williams, Andy King, Les Pratt and Jo Hole.

Many thanks to my fairy godmother Nikki Nichols.

Thank you to Thom Keep, James Moss, Aoife Larkin and Emma Marigliano of the Portico Library, Manchester for practical, friendly and ongoing encouragement. It meant a great deal to me.

To my family for their belief and support.

Thanks to John Cooper for his superb illustrations.

Thanks to Bryan Gibson, to whom I went for advice and instead came away with a publisher. Your enthusiasm, wit and vast experience helps me so very much.

Thanks and love to the cast of *'Allo 'Allo!* both here and gone.

And finally thank you to all the fans of *'Allo 'Allo!* who watched the show on television, who came to the stage show, who sent letters, or stopped us in the street to say how much they appreciated the laughs. This is for you.

Arthur Bostrom
September 2018

This book is dedicated to the memory of David Croft OBE and Jeremy Lloyd OBE, the creators and writers of *'Allo 'Allo!* and many other classic comedy series. Working with them was both a privilege and a joy. In 1985, David Croft cast me as Crabtree for the second series of *'Allo 'Allo!* and my life changed completely. I wouldn't have missed it for anything.

'A piss de resostance'
Marie Antoinette

'Can also be used as tealit pooper'
Recycling Club of Paris

'Best with rude wine'
Railway Gazette

'This book won't get you much further than Dover'
Translation Monthly

'Weak on actual French, as well as English'
Language Teachers' Review

'A fascinating case study'
Psychology Now

Disclaimer

Hello! Welcome to my book. But before we get cracking on the jolly old French lessons I just wanted a quick word. When I had the brainy idea of writing this *phrase berk* thing, I thought it might be a topping idea to have a look at some similar books and see how other authors did it. One thing I kept noticing was a page with the word 'Disclaimer' at the top. Have you seen them too? They're full of guff about this and that and well, look, here's an example:

> 'The views and opinions expressed in this book are those of the author. Readers should draw their own conclusions about any claims made or facts and opinions stated … blah blah blah …'

Still awake? I have to say that by that point my brain was starting to feel as if it was made of wool. Mind you, it has to be said that many people have made that same comparison throughout my life. Anyway, I figured that if other books had these disclaimers, mine bally well ought to as well.

So, here's my idea. If you've got any sort of beef with what I've written, whether you think it's just drivel or full of inaccuracies, then please don't badger or bother anyone about it but me. I'm the silly ass who's responsible, so if anyone is to get any flak I suppose it ought to be me. After all, I experienced an awful lot of real flak during the war, so you could say I'm used to it. So please send any complaints straight to the chappie who wrote the darned thing. I can be reached at the following address: Crabtree, France.

List of Illustrations

I arrost you in the name of the loo! *vii*
The bums are dripping! *33*
Fosh, chops and poos! Ploose! *45*
I wash I'd token the troon! *53*
Do you have willy sex? *61*
This is nit a corovon seat! *65*
Droving on the ring sod of the stroot *71*
Village Mop *72*
Has my fox arrived? *85*
A bord in the hind is worth tee in the bosh *101*
Withering Hoots *106*

Ask Crabtree

Readers will observe within the pages of this book that I, Officer Crabtree, regularly and patiently answer questions from members of the public.

Those wishing to study further examples are welcome to do so at goodmoaningfrance.com

Introduction

Hello! And welcome to my jolly little booklet designed to get you out and about (or *oot and aboot* as they say in France) while staying in that rather confusing country across the Channel.

Gosh, I found the French lessons I received in England during my training as an agent jolly hard, but it was well worth the effort. I've often seen a look of amazement on French people's faces when I speak to them, and I've come to the conclusion that it can only be because they're astonished at how well I speak their language!

I've tried to make the book as simple as possible (or *simple as pissible* as they say in France), beginning with basic everyday phrases. I hope this will give you confidence and help you feel that you're being guided by a pretty sound chap who knows a thing or two. In French that would be *a thong or tee* — I mean, could it be any easier?

Sometimes I've found that French words can be a bit jolly puzzling to some folk, and where the meaning might seem to be a bit vague, I've stuck one of those asterisk thingumajigs next to it. In case you're thinking 'What on earth's the blighter talking about?' here's an instance of where it all got a bit hot under the collar for me.

As you'd probably guess, being a secret agent means you've got to be bally careful what you say and where you say it. One day I had been given a message to pass on to someone who was staying the night in the hotel in the village. It was jolly secret and hush-hush and all that, so obviously it wasn't something I could just say in the village square!

The lady in question was ambling across the street, while I was walking my beat, so I took the opportunity to take her aside and suggest a safe rendezvous to deliver the message. Anyway, I went up to this lady and said: *'Let me tick you bock to your hotel where I will give you a massage'*. Well I mean to say, you can't be any clearer than that can you? But before I knew where I was it was like a ruddy grenade going off: she slapped my face and shrieked at me saying she'd report me to the Chief of Police. I still don't know what happened, but Rene at the café told me not to worry and that she apparently comes from Alsace. I couldn't quite figure out what that had got to do with anything but, all I'm saying is, be jolly careful out there.

Incidentally, while we're talking about all things French, it turns out that the French word for rendezvous is *rendezvous*! Extraordinary!

Okey-dokey, let's get started. First of all, I'll just describe how this book works. All right, all right … a few of you might be thinking 'Oh for goodness' sake man, we know what a bally phrase book looks like, just get on with it!' So, if you are thinking that, then my tip is to just skip along to where all the language stuff actually starts in a couple of pages time.

Now, if you're still with me, thank you for your patience. It's a funny thing, you know, but people often tell me, or at the very least they hint, that I'm not exactly loaded to the brim with the old brain cells. Well, that may well be, I couldn't say, but for those of you who, like me, enjoy taking the scenic route when picking-up a spot of new information, strap yourself in and off we go!

Most phrase books, if not all, set out the pages with words or phrases in English on the left, and the translation into French, in our case, on the right. I think this is a jolly good scheme and I'm all for it, so I decided to do the same thing. Here's an example of what I'm trying to say: imagine you're in a café or restaurant, your omelette and chips have arrived, and the condiments are on the next table. Everyone with me so far? OK, now in England you might smile at your neighbouring diners and say: 'Pass the salt please.' Now in France that would be met by either incomprehension or a Gallic shrug but, armed with this book, you can confidently say: '*Piss the silt ploose.*'

Here's how it will appear on the page:

Pass the salt please *Piss the silt ploose*

If you have a salad with your meal and you need some dressing you can call the waiter and ask for some thus:

Salad dressing *Solid drossing*
Oil *Eel*

Let's put a whole sentence together:

I nude some solid drossing. Do you have alive eel?

Now try saying it out loud. Hey Presto! (or *Hoy Prosto!*) You are now *spooking Fronch!*

Isn't it a relief to be able to order with confidence in a French restaurant? From choosing a table, to asking for the bill.

A table by the window?   *A toble by the wondow?*
A bill?   *A bull?*

Ask Crabtree

Mrs Cook from Dumbarton asks: My husband is going to be forty when we're in France. Can you suggest some *Fronch* birthday phrases to make the day go with a zip?

Crabtree: But *of curse Mme Curk*. On the day he turns *farty*, give him a shock by *washing him* a *Hippy Bathday* and throwing him a surprise *potty!*

....

Petronella from Bristol asks: We plan to be in Nouvion on Bastille Night. Should I take earplugs or will they be supplied?

Crabtree: The *bust* solution is to alter your plans and *goo there ifter.*

1

Out and About

Now this first main section of the book is a bit of a *pot-pourri* (which, strangely, is the same expression in French!). These are everyday words and phrases, so you'll always know where to look instead of having to frantically flip through the pages all the time to find the appropriate category.

There is an index (or *index)* at the end of the book, but it isn't a very good one. Or helpful either. Sorry.

Anyway, imagine you've just stepped off the boat and you want to speak French to someone.

Hello!	*Good moaning*
Good day	*Good moaning*
Good morning	*Good moaning*
Good afternoon	*Good moaning*
How are you?	*Hoo are you?**
What is your name?	*Wit is your nome?*
How far are the shops?	*Hoo fur are the ships?*
What a lovely day!	*Wit a lively do!*

---

* There could be some misunderstanding here.

What a windy day!	*Wit a wondy do!*
Follow me please	*Fallow moo ploose*
Where shall we go now?	*War shall we goo noo?*
Look!	*Lick!*
I was just passing	*I was just pissing*
A drop of rain	*A drip of rune*
Plenty of sun today!	*Plonty of sin to do!*
I am completely lost	*I am complotely list*
Which way?	*Watch woo?*
Down the street	*Doon the stroot*
Forty francs	*Farty fronks**

In case you weren't aware, all this malarkey with French came about because I was stationed undercover as a *poloceman* in the Normandy village of Nouvion. Apparently, a lot of people know this because there was some chappie filming the whole thing! I can't say I ever noticed. Anyway, I'd never been a *poloceman* before, but, I don't know, in the end you pick up the thread of things, don't you? Plus, I'm very tall, which helped a bit I suppose. Obviously, I had to brush up on my schoolboy French pretty jolly quickly though, so apart from the above everyday phrases I had quite a few which dealt with everyday situations in war. They're in the next bit, I hope that you won't need any of these, but, as I can be a funny old thing when the mood takes me, I include them for sentimental reasons, and historical interest!

---

* Yes, I know they're euros now. Just call me an old-fashioned fool!

Ask Crabtree

Mrs Jean Blatherwick from Bungay asks: Is it really necessary to talk French in France? Surely everyone speaks English these days?

Crabtree: *Minny purple* do *spook Onglish* but I personally think it *pollute* to *spook Fronch* or at least to *mook an attompt*. I know from people's reactions when I *spook the Fronch longwodge* that they *approoshiate* my *offort*. Also, when I *spook* I find people often smile, or even *collapse* into *holpless lifter*. People are so *frondly!*

....

Mrs Joanne Pargeter from Billericay asks: We've been invited to a wedding in France and I'm worried I won't know what to say. Any suggestions Crabtree?

Crabtree: *Relox Mme Purgeter*! It's simple enough. There is the *brode* and *greem*, *bust min*, *brodesmoods*, *mither* and *fother of the brode* and *mither* and *fother of the greem*. If you're at a loss and wonder what to say to French guests just point and say: '*Wit a winderful wadding cack*!' Really, how can they not be impressed?

A POLOCEMAN'S NEWT BERK (1)

At the police station in Nouvion I was issued with a notebook, and on the opposite page is a copy of my first day of note-taking on the job. As a bit of added fun, I've included a few randomly selected pages from my notebooks over the years I served in Nouvion during the war.

You'll see more of these as you progress through this *phrase berk*. My aim is both to entertain you with a glimpse of the daily life of a French *poloceman*, but also to encourage you as you study.

Through reading my notes, selected from different times, you'll be able to see how quickly I became a master of the language, and therefore how quickly you can achieve the same.

The year was *nuneteen-farty-win* and the month was *Moo*. I challenge any secret agent getting very far on foreign soil without at least knowing those two facts!

Numbers

One	*Win*	Six	*Sex*
Two	*Tee*	Seven	*Siven*
Three	*Threw*	Eight	*Oat*
Four	*Far*	Nine	*Nune*
Five	*Fave*	Ten	*Tin*

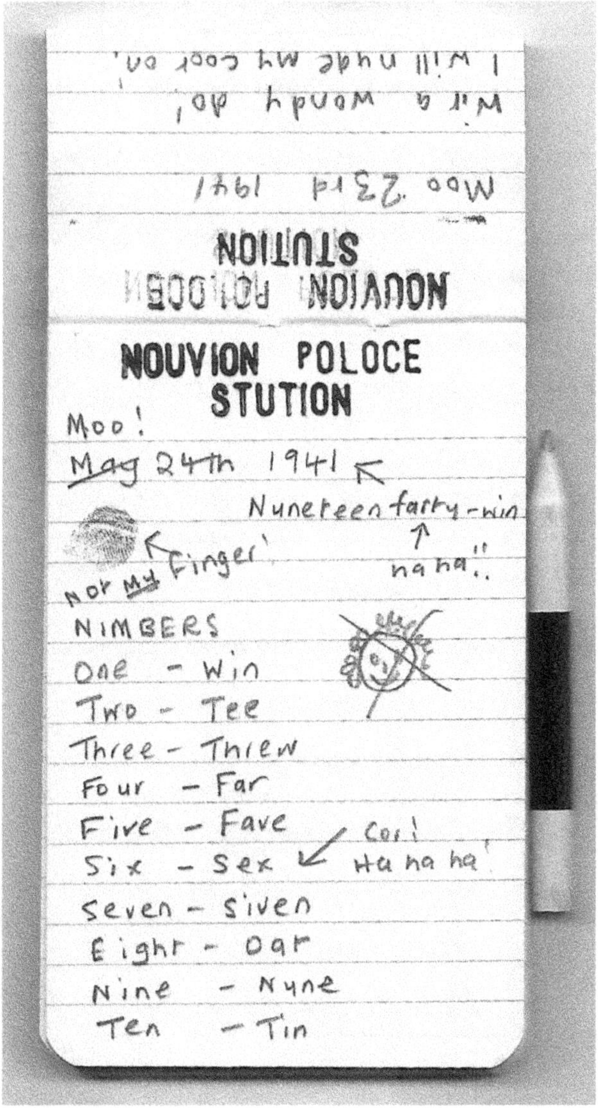

A POLOCEMAN'S NEWT BERK

(upside down at top:)
Moo 23rd 1941
Wit a Wondy do!
I Will nude my coot on.

NOUVION POLOCE STUTION *(stamped, upside down)*

NOUVION POLOCE STUTION

Moo!

May 24th 1941

Nuneteen farty-win
ha ha!!

← Finger
Not My

NIMBERS
One — Win
Two — Tee
Three — Thiew
Four — Far
Five — Fave
Six — Sex ← Cor! Ha ha ha!
Seven — Siven
Eight — Oar
Nine — Nyne
Ten — Tin

Ask Crabtree

Barry Cuckfield from Walthamstow asks: I'm a student and me and a few mates are thinking of going to Paris for the day. What do you suggest Crabtree?

Crabtree: There are a *nimber* of *hip-on, hip-off* tours where you get on a boat or a bus and see the city. Or you could queue to go up the *Awful Tour* and see the whole of *Poris*. If you have *tome*, you could *witch* a cabaret and see *Con Con dincing*. By the *woo*, the *French* word for cabaret is *cabaret!* Crazy!

....

Edna from Barnsley asks: My Stan goes t'ot match ivry Satdi an supps hissen under t'table when they loise. They 'av t'beer in t'France, or what love?

Crabtree: *Odna, wit longwodge* are you *spooking ploose*?

....

Amelia Salt of Pangbourne asks: I work in a charity shop at weekends and have accumulated a stock of French maps from the 1930s. Has anything changed or will I find them useful?

Crabtree: *Mme Silt*, every *thong* has changed. As antiques though they may be worth something for *ruddy cosh*.

2

Wartime Phrases

What a big bang!	*Wit a bog bing!*
Are bombs dropping?	*Are bums dripping?*
Keep away from the windows!	*Koop awoo from the wondows!*
Look! Parachutes!	*Lick! Parashits!*
I think I've been shot	*I thonk I've been shat*
Put that light out!	*Pat that loot oot!*
I hear a tank	*I whore a tink*
What time is curfew?	*Wit tome is corfu?*
Bullet-proof vest	*Ballot-preef vast*
Get ready to fight!	*Git ruddy to fart!*
Let's go into battle!	*Let's goo unto bottle!*
Battleship	*Bottleshop*
Enemy tank	*Onomy tink*
Submarine	*Sobmaroon*
Blackout blinds	*Blickoot blonds*
Resistance fighter	*Resostance farter*
Copping some flak	*Kipping some flock*
The Last Post	*The Lost Pist*
Back to Blighty	*Bick to Bloaty*
Air Force	*Oar Farce*
Enemy at the gates	*Onomy at the goats*

Luftwaffe	*Leftwiffer*
Hitler	*Hotler*
Ration book	*Russian berk*
Spy network	*Spa nutwick*
Mole	*Mule*
Anti-aircraft guns	*Auntie-earcroft gins*

I hope that's given you an idea of some of the expressions I had to translate at the drop of a hat during the war. I sincerely hope you won't have any need of them during your stay in France but, as the saying goes, *'You nover noo!'*

WARTIME PHRASES

A POLOCEMAN'S NEWT BERK (2)

Gosh. What an absolute corker of a day! Everyone in Nouvion went absolutely crackers. Everybody that is except the Germans. Not a sign of Herr Flick, Helga, the Colonel or Gruber. Perhaps they slid off with their tails between their legs in Gruber's little tank.

Rene had a victory party at the café, with all the Resistance people there. I was part of that of course, but I didn't recognise most of them. Yvette gave me a kiss. Mimi tried, but unfortunately she couldn't reach.

Victory Phrases

Their tails between their legs
Their tools betwoon their logs

A day off
A do off

Charles de Gaulle
Chorles de Gool

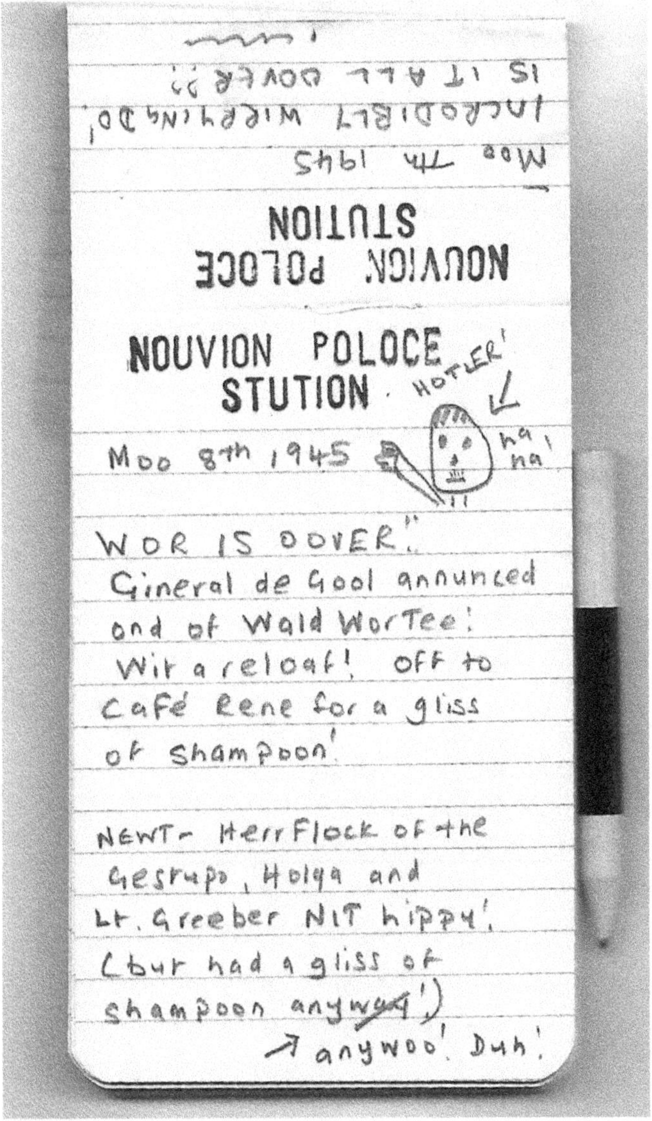

(upside-down at top:)
"IncRODIBLY WiRRYING Do!
IS IT ALL OOVER??"

Moo 7th 1945

NOUVION POLOCE STUTION

NOUVION POLOCE STUTION. HOTLER!

Moo 8th 1945   ha! ha!

WOR IS OOVER!!
Gineral de Gool annunced ond of Wald WorTee! Wit a reloaf! off to Café Rene for a gliss of shampoon!

NEWT - HerrFlick of the Gestupo, Holga and Lt. Greeber NIT hippy! (but had a gliss of shampoon anywuq!)
→ anywoo! Duh!

Ask Crabtree

Spike from Blackpool asks: I have heard a rumour that they don't have chip shops in France?

Crabtree: *Sodly* it is *moostly tree!*

....

Archie from Yeovil Asks: I'm told some French motorways go on for ever. Is it as bad as the A303?

Crabtree: No *rood* in the *whool weerld* is as *bod* as the A303.

....

Mr Smith of Wearside asks: I don't get out much these days, so I am wondering how the vast expanse of the French countryside might affect me. Last time I looked across a field I got all dizzy.

Crabtree: I would suggest *tick* it one *fold at a tome*. If you start to feel *dazzy* then return to *Ongland*. At least you will have *treed*.

3

French Language Rules

If you were taught as I was, at a minor public school in the Home Counties of England (and, not to disparage the old dump too much, but it jolly well *was* 'minor') then you probably came out of French lessons feeling dizzy, clueless or bored. Or in my case, a combination of all three.

French masters as a breed aren't particularly known for their joviality, and at St Werburgh's we had a particularly un-jolly French master by the name of Banstead (or *Monsieur Banstead* as he insisted on calling himself). He was certainly un-jolly for yours truly anyway! Here's an example of the sort of thing that was thrown my way pretty well every day in class:

Monsieur Banstead: Crabtree! What's the French for 'cloth-eared nitwit'?
Me: I don't know, Sir!
Monsieur Banstead: Boys, could that be because Crabtree *is* a cloth-eared nitwit? (*Sound of braying boys' laughter*).

Of course, I now know it's *clith-eared notwot*, but it's probably too late to surprise old Banstead now!

To be fair to the old buzzard though, he did teach us all the rudiments of the *French longwodge*, and I suppose he was responsible for lighting the fuse and producing the fluent *French spooker* that I am today.

We did use to rag old Banstead sometimes, in the way schoolboys do: flicking ink-soaked blotting paper at him with a ruler when he had his back to us and other capers. More often than not it was me who got caught and sent to the headmaster for six-of-the-best. Maybe that taught me to be cleverer when I was a secret agent in France during the war.

I realise that schoolchildren may well use this book to help them improve their *French* so, here are a few words and phrases that might be of help.

School Words

Desk	*Dusk*
Blotting paper	*Blatting pooper*
Ink	*Onk*
Ruler	*Reeler*
Grammar	*Grimmer*
Gymnastics	*Jamnostics*
Staff	*Stiff*
Headmaster	*Hodmister*
Six-of-the-best	*Sex-of-the-bust**

---

* Thankfully none of you will have to experience this anymore.

4

My Everyday Practice

Just in case you've been getting a bit nervous about all the learning and practice you'll have to do when getting to grips with this language, let me show you how I managed it when I was parachuted into Normandy in France during WW2. I was from British Intelligence Headquarters (in French: *Brutish Intolligence Headquitters*) and so although I knew enough French to begin with (I suppose that was in some way thanks to *Monsieur Banstead!*) I had to learn to be well-understood pretty quickly.

My disguise was as a *poloceman*, and there was good reason for that. In fact, I remember one of the first things I said to the group of jolly resistance members who found me hanging from a tree in the woods outside Nouvion, where I landed:

'I have disgeesed as a poloceman, so that I am oble to mauve aboot with complate frodom'.

Even now I don't see how I could have put it any clearer!

My Daily Routine

It was hard to have any regularity during those old days as a secret agent in the war. One minute I'd be walking the village streets pretending to be a *polocéman* and the next I'd be dressed as a Can-Can girl for some crazy resistance plan. When life wasn't hair-raising though I was up at seven, quick rinse, Shredded Wheat or cornflakes (dropped by Spitfire) and a cup of tea and off and out into the mayhem. As for eating during the day I'd pop in at the back door of *Café Rene* and they'd give me a potted rabbit or a bowl of fishbone soup, or whatever they'd found to cook.

Sometimes villagers would give me a wink in the street and produce a package of something delicious to eat. I think it was their way of saying 'Thank you' for all the dangerous work I was doing as a resistance fighter. Jolly moving really, if you think about it, but anyway I managed to keep body and soul together and for the most part was fit as a fiddle.

Shredded Wheat	*Shrodded Wait*
Cornflakes	*Curnflukes*
Potted rabbit	*Patted robbit*
Fishbone soup	*Foshbune soap*
A wink in the street	*A wonk in the stroot*
Package	*Pickage*
Resistance fighter	*Resostance farter*
Body and soul	*Biddy and sole*
Fit as a fiddle	*Fat as a fuddle*
Spitfire	*Spotfear*

5

Everyday Words and Phrases

So: back to today. Next is a list of everyday words: the sort one might need to use any time. Here's a tip: why not, just for a bit of practice, write out these words and phrases on a piece of paper and keep it in your jacket or coat pocket for when you need them!

Objects

Table	*Toble*
Chair	*Chore*
Front door	*Front deer*
Knocker	*Knicker**
Trousers	*Troosers*
Hat	*Hit**
Motor car	*Mewter cur*
Lamp	*Lump*
Lump	*Limp*
Limp	*Lamp*
Pump	*Pimp**
Book	*Berk*

---

* Take care to avoid misunderstandings!

Pamphlet	*Pimphlet*
Newspaper	*Nosepooper*
Lookout post	*Lickout pist*
Bottle of wine	*Bittle of ween*

Let's see if we can use some of these words we've learned so far to make an actual sentence — or two.

Good moaning! Ploose may I hov a kippy of the dooly nosepooper?

How did you do? Just for fun, I slipped in a couple of new words there: *'kippy'* and *'dooly'*, which, of course, mean 'copy' and 'daily'. But what is the French for the name of your favourite daily newspaper? Here's a list.

Newspapers

The Times	*The Tomes*
The Sunday Times	*The Sandy Tomes*
The Daily Mail	*The Dooly Mole*
The Telegraph	*The Tollygruff*
The Independent	*The Independent*
The Sun	*The Sin*
Daily Mirror	*Dooly Marrow*
The Guardian	*The Gruniodd*
Huffington Post	*Hoffington Pist*

Everyday Conversational Words

Lucky	*Licky*
Bad person	*Bod parson*
Good person	*Gid parson*
Policeman	*Poloceman*
Shopkeeper	*Shipkooper*
Chemist	*Cummist*
Battle	*Bottle*
Language	*Longwodge*
French	*Fronch*
British	*Brutish*
Laugh	*Liff*
Cough	*Cuff*
Splutter	*Splatter*
Kissing	*Cussing*
Big	*Bog*
Small	*Smell*

OK let's try another couple of sentences!!

Is that poloceman cussing the cummist?
Noo. I thonk he's just cuffing and splattering!

Not an everyday phrase perhaps. But it might be useful one day.

OK so you've arrived somewhere in France and you feel a bit peckish or possibly just thirsty. You walk into a bar or a café. What on earth do you say to the waiter? Choose from this list and order with confidence!!

Food and Beverage

Food	*Feed*
Beverage	*Boverage*
Drink	*Drunk*
Cake	*Cack*
Shortbread	*Shitbrod*
Éclair	*Éclair**
Sponge fingers	*Spinge fungus*
Bread and butter	*Brod and bitter*
Apple pie and cream	*Ipple poo and chrome*
Meat pie	*Moot poo*
Cornish pasty	*Curnish pisty*
Omelette	*Omelette†*
Scrambled eggs	*Scrimbled oggs*
Lamb chops	*Limb chips*
Mashed potatoes	*Mushed potutoes*
Peas	*Poos‡*
Frogs legs	*Frigs logs*
Fish and chips	*Fosh and chops§*
Beer-battered cod	*Bore-buttered cad*
Fish fingers	*Fosh fungus*
Pot of tea	*Pit of two*
Pint of beer	*Punt of bore*
Glass of water	*Gloss of witter*

---

* Same word! Weird!
† Same word! Staggering!
‡ Take care with this as it can also mean 'pies'.
§ For some reason this works perfectly well in New Zealand too!

So, let's put some of these words together in a conversation you might have in a French café.

> **You:** *I would lick a poo.*
> **Waiter:** *Wit kind of poo? Moot? Choose and innion? Stook and kadney?*
> **You:** *No think you. I am winting a padding!*
> **Waiter:** *Ah! Would you lick an ipple poo? With whopped chrome?*
> **You:** *Sounds toasty! And a pit of two for tee.*
> **Waiter:** *No priblem.*
> **You:** *And a bull whenover you're ruddy.*

Followed that all right? Doesn't it just fill you with confidence?

Ask Crabtree

Douglas from Inverurie asks: Is it possible to find porridge in France?

Crabtree: I have never seen a *bool of eatmole* in all my years in *Fronce*. If you want *porridge*, then I suggest you *brung* your *oon*. You could then take your *bool of eatmole* into the hotel restaurant and ask them to *hoot it*.

But what if you've booked a holiday cottage in France? You'll want to know all the correct words for things in the home. Here they are.

In the Home

House	*Hoose*
Mouse	*Moose*
Mousetrap	*Moosetrip*
Sink	*Sunk*
Stove	*Steve*
Pots and pans	*Pats and pins*
Knives and forks	*Knaves and fucks**
Double bed	*Dibble bod*
King size	*Kong says*
Bed linen	*Bod lenin*
Bath taps	*Borth tips*
Soap	*Soup*
Toothpaste	*Teethpist*
Shampoo	*Shompee*
Table and chairs	*Toble and chores*
Washing machine	*Wishing mushoon*
Living room	*Loving room*†
Dining-room	*Duning-reem*
Bedroom	*Bodreem*
Bathroom	*Borthreem*
Porch	*Perch*

---

* Take care using this with children and the very elderly.
† This might be misunderstood by some people. Particularly newly-weds.

Loft	*Lift*
Lift	*Loft*
Upstairs	*Ipstores*
Ceiling	*Soiling*
Floor	*Flair*
Toilet paper	*Tealit pooper*
Laundry basket	*Loondry biscuit*

Let's have a go at another few sentences. Here's a conversation that could occur at any time in the home.

Person 1: *There is noo tealit pooper in the borthreem!*
Person 2: (Shooting) *There are several reels ipstores in the lift. Lick there!*
Person 1: *Ookey-dookey! There's plonty of soup, but we nude to buy more teethpist.*

All right, I know I sneaked in a couple of new words, but I'm sure you soon got the hang of it. Try it out on the family one night and see who's able to understand!

A POLOCEMAN'S NEWT BERK (3)

NOUVION POLOCE STUTION

December
December 25TH 1941

who nocked my ponci!
snoofluke!

Chrostmas Do!
Hippy Chrostmas Everybiddy!
Chrostmas troo

new words —
Gravy - Groovy
Roast chicken - Roost chuckin
A way in a manger
— Awoo in a minger.
Crackers - Crockers
(I ♥ Yvette!)
← a dog secret!

Here's another page from my *newt berk* and this time it's from Christmas 1941. Although I was never really officially off duty, I remember I had a quick walk about the village and then spent the rest of the day at *Café Rene*. The kitchen had managed to roast a few chickens which were served with potatoes and carrots. The Germans had the white meat off the breast of course while the rest of us had the dark. But somehow the French have a knack of making the most unlikely food taste alright!

In the evening Madame Edith did her cabaret, mostly singing carols. Of course, as usual, she was completely out of tune, so everyone joined in to drown her out. I must admit, I'm a bit red-faced about my silly comment about Yvette. It's all a long time ago, but she was a bit of a corker!

Christmas Words

Happy Christmas	*Hippy Chrostmas*
Christmas Tree	*Chrostmas Troo*
Christmas Do	*Chrostmas Do*
Gravy	*Groovy*
Roast Chicken	*Roost Chuckin*
Crackers	*Crockers*
Snowflake	*Snoofluke*
Away in a Manger	*Awoo in a Minger*
Silent Night	*Salent Newt*

6

Going on Holiday to France

Now I'm sure a few of you are getting a bit hot under the collar and saying 'When's this blasted chap going to teach us something useful? I don't need to know the word for "toothpaste"!!'

Well I feel your pain, or *fool your poon,* as they say over the water, but I think it's important to be relaxed and get the sense of a language before delving too far into specifics. So, this part of the book is probably going to be the most well-thumbed for most of you.

So, what sort of holiday are you going on?

Reader: That's none of your darned business! Get on with it man!
Me: All right! All right!

Essentials

Passport — *Pissport*
Tickets — *Tockets*
Booking confirmation — *Berking confumotion*
Bank card — *Bonk curd*

Travel money	*Trivvle minny*
Luggage	*Liggage*
Bag	*Bog*
Laptop	*Liptap*
Ipad	*Ipod*
Ipod	*Ipad*
Adapter	*Adopter*
Headphones	*Hodphoons*
Guide book	*Goad berk*
Maps	*Mops*
Insurance documents	*Inseerance dickuments*
Book to read	*Berk to rood*

At the Airport or Ferry

Check-in desk	*Chock-on dusk*
Luggage trolley	*Liggage trilley*
Passport Control	*Pissport Cantrale*
Duty free	*Dirty froo*
Departure lounge	*Deporture lunge*
Departure gate	*Deporture goat*
Cross channel ferry	*Criss chunnel fairy*
Vehicle deck	*Vayickle duck*
Hovercraft	*Hoovercroft*
Hydrofoil	*Hodrafeel*
Lifeboat	*Loafbait*
Life jacket	*Loaf jicket*

Ask Crabtree

Mrs Maureen Barber from Tiverton asks: My family is planning a trip to France and we all have different ideas about how to get there. My husband wants to fly, I want to go by train, and my young son Liam wants to go by ferry. What do you suggest, Crabtree?

Crabtree: I would *goo by fairy*. A *loaf on the acean woves* for *moo every tome!* The whole business of flying is so *strossful,* and going by *troon* under the *Chunnel* means up to half-an-hour in *dickness!* Give your young son a thrill and *goo by boot*.

....

Stanley Bucknall from Paignton asks: My partner and I love travelling by train. Is train travel a good way to see the country?

Crabtree: It is a *winderful woo* to *soo Fronce!* There are *troons gooing* almost *overywhore*. There are *hay spode troons* to most of the *boggest coties* and *brunch lones gooing* to *smeller toons*. If you like *troonspitting* then go to big cities like *Poris*. *Hippy troon trivelling!*

Now what about clothes? To make things simpler, and quicker for the single traveller, I've divided the list between men and women. I do hope I haven't left anything out, ladies!

Clothes for Men

Underwear	*Inderwore*
Socks	*Secks**
Shorts	*Shirts*
Shirts	*Shorts*
Trousers	*Troosers*†
Sweater	*Swatter*
Swimming-trunks	*Swarming-trinks*
Flip-flops	*Flop-flaps*
Hat for sun	*Hot for sin*‡
Light jacket	*Lute jicket*

Clothes for Women

Dresses	*Drosses*
Skirts	*Skairts*§
Lingerie	*Lingerie*¶
Tops	*Taps*
Necklace	*Nockless*
Coat	*Coot*
Bikini	*Bukunu*
Bra	*Bree*
Stockings	*Stickings*

---

* Care needed when pronouncing this word.
† This also works in Scotland for some reason.
‡ There can be misunderstandings with this.
§ This can be useful in Liverpool too.
¶ I know! The same word! Extraordinary!

Nightgown	*Newtgoon*
Silk nightie	*Sulk newty*

Everything Else

Backpack	*Bickpick*
Mobile phone	*Mubile phoon*
Sunglasses	*Singlosses*
Toilet bag	*Tealit bog*
Shaving kit	*Shoving cat*
Roll-on deodorant	*Rail-in doyadeeront*
Sun cream	*Sin chrome*
First aid kit	*Fast ode cat*
Medicinal drugs	*Medocinal dregs*
Ear plugs	*Oar plegs*

On the Beach

Bucket and spade	*Bicket and spode*
Fishing net	*Foshing nut*
Sun lounger	*Sin lunger*
Deck chair	*Duck chore*
Bathing hut	*Boothing hat*
Boating lake	*Booting lurk*
Coral reef	*Carol roof*
Tide	*Toad*
Jellyfish	*Jollyfosh*

SPF forty-five	*SPF farty-fave*
Picnic basket	*Packnick biscuit*
Ice cream	*Ace chrome*
Lollipop	*Lillipoop*
Fruit squash	*Freet squish*
Beach baby wrap	*Birch booby rip*
Beach towel	*Birch tool*
Toddler sunglasses	*Tiddler singlosses*
Airbed/LiLo	*Oarbod/LoLi*
Bodyboard	*Biddybird*
Snorkel/Fin	*Snurkel/Fan*
Wet wipes	*Wot woops*

Helpful Phrases for a Beach Holiday

Is the main beach sandy or rocky?
Is the moon birch sindy or ricky?

Which is the way to the beach?
Watch is the woo to the birch?

Is the water cold?
Is the witter killed?

I just want to paddle.
I jist want to piddle.

(For families with babies)
Do you have cribs?
Do you have crabs?*

I need to buy postcards and a strawberry lollipop.
I nude to buy pistcurds and a strewborry lillipap.

Is the tide coming in?
Is the toad coming on?

I would like to rent a boat, please.
I would lick to runt a boot, ploose.

Is there a small paddling pool?
Is there a smell piddling pole?

I am looking for the docks.
I am licking for the dicks.

(If you need to inflate an airbed)
Do you have a pump?
Do you have a pimp?†

Please rub some cream on my back.
Ploose rib some chrome on my bick.

---

* Careful with this.
† Careful with this as well as some people may take offence.

Ok, but what if you wanted to go on a walking or hiking holiday? You're probably going to need lots of different things. I've never been much of a strenuous walker type myself to be honest. I don't mind an amble down to the duck pond or a walk around the block to limber up, but I leave walking the length of the River Seine, or climbing Mont Blanc, to hardier souls!

Here is all you need.

Packing for a Walking Holiday

Rucksack	*Ricksock*
Walking-boots	*Wicking-boats*
Waterproof jacket	*Witterproof jacket*
Woolly socks	*Willy sex*[*]
Woolly hat	*Willy hut*[†]
Woolly sweater	*Willy swatter*[‡]
Map	*Mop*
Sleeping-bag	*Slooping-bog*
Compass	*Campiss*
Gas stove	*Gus steve*
Small torch	*Smell titch*
Multi-purpose tool	*Malty-porpoise tail*
Tent	*Tint*
Plates and cutlery	*Pleats and catlery*
Assorted plasters	*Asserted plisters*
Antiseptic cream	*Intisoptic chrome*

---

[*] For some reason this phrase can cause confusion and, sometimes, offence.
[†] Ditto.
[‡] Ditto.

Ask Crabtree

Barney Overton from Llantwit Major asks: My family loves watersports of all kinds. Would France be suitable for us do you think?

Crabtree: Of *curse* it *wid! Fronce* is *winderful* for *witterspurts!* The coast is fantastic for *yitting* and *soafing the woves.* The more adventurous could try *coat-soafing.* There is also *doving* and *swarming* — but if you get tired at the end of the day you can always go for a *piddle!*

....

Mrs Cynthia Drake from Surbiton asks: My husband and I aren't really interested in food, restaurants or the seaside. Our main interest is Art. Do you have any suggestions for us?

Crabtree: I'm not really the chappie to ask about *Urt*, *Mme Droke*, as the only painting I know of is "The Fallen Madonna with the Big Boobies" by Van Klomp, or, as we'd say in *Fronch:* "The *Follen Madinna* with the *Bog Beebies*" by *Von Klimp*. The last time I saw it, it is was hidden in a *knockwurst* sausage, but for all I know it may now be in an *Urt Gillery. Hippy hinting!*

Of course, 'sightseeing' isn't nearly as strenuous, but can be very pleasurable. Here's a handy list of words and phrases that will help you out whether you're in Paris, the French Alps or the docks at Marseille.

Sightseeing

English	French
Eiffel Tower	*Awful Tour*
Chateau	*Chateau**
Castle	*Kistle*
Monastery	*Ministry*
Vineyard	*Van yard*
Tour guide	*Tire goad*
Postcards	*Pistcurds*
Docks	*Dicks*†
Coach trip	*Couch trap*
River cruise	*Rover craze*
Lookout point	*Lickout pint*
Ferry trip	*Fairy trap*
High speed train	*Hay spode troon*
Medieval town	*Maddyoval toon*

Camping and Caravanning Holidays

Ever since the war there seems to have been a huge increase in people going camping and caravanning for their holidays. It certainly costs less

---

* For some reason it's the same word as English!
† This word has been known to give offence, so do take care!

GOING ON HOLIDAY TO FRANCE

than a hotel and there's lots of choice where to go. In recent years France has become a major destination. Here are a few extra words and phrases that might help you if you're planning to spend some time under canvas, or in your own home from home: a towing caravan or motorhome.

Cross channel ferry	*Criss chunnel fairy*
Customs	*Cistoms*
Passport Check	*Pissport Chock*
Caravan	*Corovon*
Motorhome	*Mooterhume*
Caravan site	*Corovon seat*
Caravan seat	*Corovon site*
Pitch fees	*Patch fuse*
Six berth	*Sex bath**
Outfit	*Eatfat*
Caravan heater	*Corovon hooter*
Battery	*Buttery*
Awning	*Earning*
Hitch	*Hutch*
Hitch lock	*Hutch lick*
Nose weight	*News wart*
Wheel lock	*Whale lick*
Snaking	*Sneaking*
Jockey wheel	*Jacky whale*
Pop top	*Poop tap*

---

* Once again, care needed, as some people might be confused and think you were talking about socks.

Here's a few more for the campers.

Mains hookup	*Means hiccup*
Tinted window	*Tainted wondow*
Bedside lamp	*Bodside lump*
Satellite television	*Sitalot tollyvision*
Blackout blinds	*Blickoot blonds*
Tent	*Tint*
Tent pole	*Tint pool*
Airbed	*Earbod*
Sleeping bag	*Slooping bog*
Pegs	*Pigs**
Mallet	*Millet*†
Camping chairs	*Kimping chores*
Cooking utensils	*Kicking utonsils*
Cutlery	*Catlery*
Gas bottle	*Gus bittle*
Stove	*Steve*

---

* Confusion can sometimes arise when using this word in conversations with farmers or butchers.
† Similarly, avoid misunderstanding by not using this word in a pet store, or anywhere near parrots, cockatoos or budgerigars. With canaries, use your own judgment.

A POLOCEMAN'S NEWT BERK (4)

Here we are with another example from my *poloceman's newt berk*.

As you can see from the date, *Jean the farth,* this was written quite a while after the last example. By this time, I had begun a 'Daily Diary', listing some of the activities I got up to during my working day.

Ten out of ten, I think, for writing clear sentences in French, but I was a bit of a clot for talking about the Resistance in a note book that could be read by anyone. Including Germans!

Which new words and expressions do we learn here?

Everyday Words

Daily diary	*Dooley dairy*
German	*Jawmen*
Crimes	*Creams*
Beans on toast	*Boons on toost*
Meeting	*Mooting*

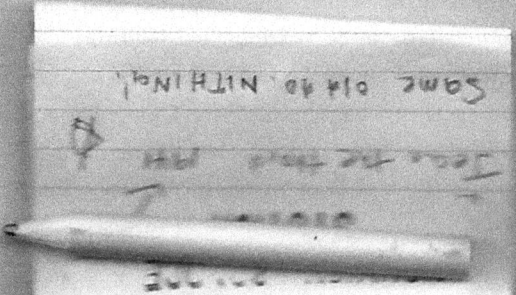

NOUVION POLOCE STUTION

← 10/10

Jean the farth (Froday)
DOOLEY DAIRY

Todoo I wicked aroond Nouvion on my poloceman's dirty roond. Jawmen's everywore! No-one from the goneral piblic had commuted any creams!

3pm. Fooling puckish! Wont to Café René. I asked Yvette for "BOONS ON TOOST," But she did nit knew wirl was ticking aboot! Iatte ond had "hom and ogg!" Michelle came in and wanted a tip secret mooting in berk room!

✻ Moby I should nit mention this?? ✻

Now you may have noticed that this book has some illustrations in cartoon form of me in the process of doing my daily duty. Over the years I patrolled the streets of Nouvion, I had often noticed a chap with a sketch book around, but he always kept his distance. On the few occasions when I decided to find out what he was up to, the blighter always 'disappeared like a phantom into the night', as my old Resistance colleague Michelle would have said.

He seemed to have disappeared after the war and only re-appeared recently, looking much older, which I suppose was to be expected. I doubt I look quite as youthful as I once did either. Anyway, it turned out that he'd got wind of my *phrase berk* idea and accosted me when I was having a quick coffee in *Café Rene*. It turned out his name was *Monsieur Jean Coupaire* and he was a freelance illustrator. He'd been working in Paris for many years doing court sketches of those blighters in criminal trials and had recently retired and returned to Nouvion. It turned out he had loads of drawings. I asked him why he had done so many of me and he said he just found something about the way I went about my *poloceman's* business very funny. I asked him what was particularly funny, but he didn't seem to want to elaborate so I *let it piss*, as we say in France. But he was so grateful for all the sketching practice I'd given him that he gave me them all for free. I bought him a small cognac, we shook hands and that was that.

But it made me think that, while being involved with the police is probably not foremost on your mind when considering a holiday in France, it might happen. Obviously, with all my years as a *poloceman*, I know a fair bit about the law over here. If you were unfortunate enough to meet me, or one of my colleagues, during a policing incident, I would be failing in my duties* as a *phrase berk* writer if I didn't give you some warning of what you might be in for!

Meeting a Policeman

'Ello 'Ello!
'Allo 'Allo!

I arrest you in the name of the law!
I arrost you in the nome of the loo!

You are nicked!
You are knocked!

You are looking to spend a night behind bars!
You are licking to spend a newt behind bores!

You had better come with me.
You had butter come with moo.

Now that you're becoming, I hope, an advanced student, I'm going to provide, in French, a list solely concerned with crime. See how many you can understand.

---

* Or *fooling* in my *dirties*, as we say in France!

French Words Concerning Crime

Cream
Cream of pission
Bigglary
Bigglary with minaces
Disturbing the puss
Droving on the ring sod of the stroot
Droving with felty lutes
Drunk droving
Porking on a zobra crissing
Foolure to poo a porking fone
Joywicking
Codnipping
Handbog snitching
Fooling to stip at a rod lute
Assilt and buttery
Brooch of the puss
Trosspiss
Hay trooson
Potty trooson
Escoop from custardy
Contompt of curt
*Imitooting a poloceman**

How did you do? Needless to say, I hope none of you ever commit any of the above *creams* when you're in France!

---

* Of course, I did this myself for a number of years, but it was all part of the war effort!

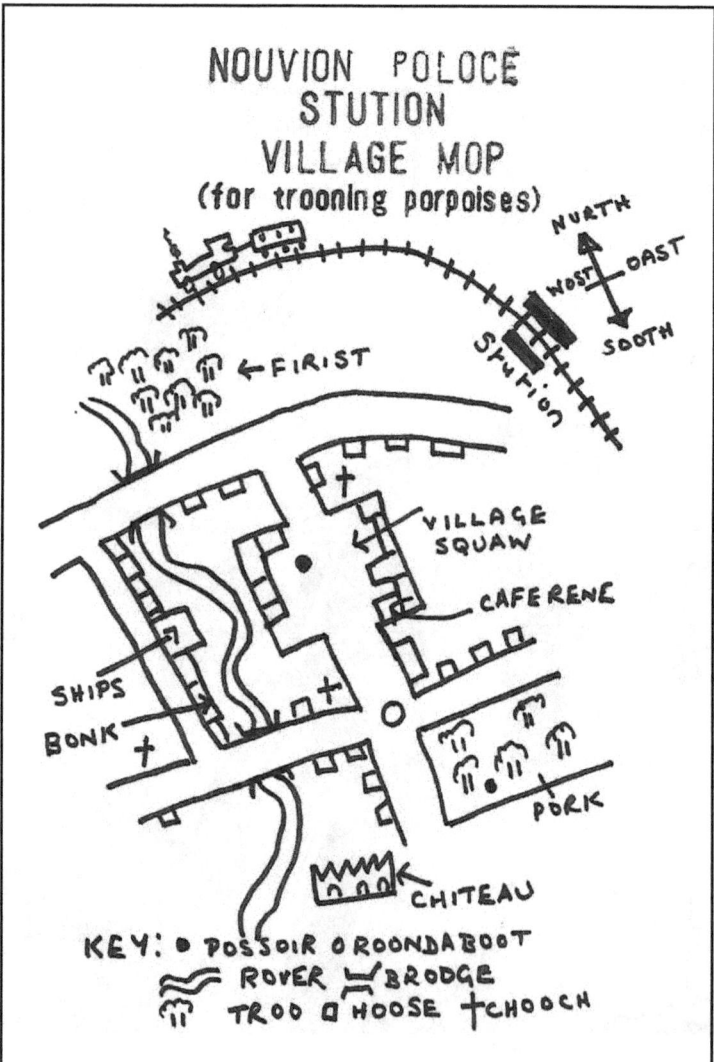

7

All About Banking

OK everyone, back to everyday things on holiday.

One of the things most people appear to get in a complete fog about is money: the exchange rate seems to change every day, and banks and post offices are very different from those at home.

This next section should help!

> Are you involved in banking?
> *Are you involved in bonking?*
>
> Will my British bank card work here?
> *Will my Brutish bonk curd wick whore?*
>
> Please show me where to bank.
> *Ploose show moo where to bonk.*
>
> I need to withdraw some cash.
> *I nude to withdrear some cosh.*

I think you'll agree: they are useful phrases that you'll doubtless use often. Here are a few words that will also help you to manage your money while away in France.

Bank manager	*Bonk minniger*
Bank teller	*Bonk tiller*
Traveller's cheque	*Triveller's chock*
Bank pass book	*Bonk piss berk*
Euro	*Eerie*
Pound	*Pond*
Scottish pound	*Skittish pond*
40p	*Farty poo*
Dollar	*Della*
Rouble	*Rubble*
Travel money	*Trivel minny*
Stocks and bonds	*Sticks and bands*
Overdraft	*Ooverdrift*
Cash machine	*Cosh moshoon*
Eurozone	*Eeriezoon*
Percentage rate	*Pissontage root*

8

Shopping

OK, so assuming you've successfully managed the above words and phrases and now you've *minny in your picket*: what to spend it on?

Most people seem to find shopping an enjoyable pastime, but it can be a source of stress when abroad. Here are a few sections about all aspects of shopping on holiday in France, with lists of the different kinds of shops, and a selection of words to help you find and buy what you're looking for.

Let's begin with some useful phrases:

> Where is the fitting room please?
> *Wore is the fatting ream ploose?*

> I am looking for the latest fashion.
> *I am licking for the lootest fish in.**

> These trousers are too short.
> *These troosers are too shirt.*

---

* Some people, on using this phrase, have been directed to the nearest harbour. I can't explain why, but it's one of those odd things that can happen when you're on holiday!

This shirt feels too big for me.
This short fools too bog for moo.

Forty pounds? Is there any discount?
Farty ponds? Is there onny descant?

Which is your biggest sized lamp?
Watch is your boggest seized lump?

Excuse me, where do I pay?
Excuse moo, where do I pee?

Please direct me to your crockery department.
Ploose diroct moo to your crackery deportment.

Useful Words for Clothes Shopping

Cotton	*Kitten*
Silk	*Sulk*
Wool	*Will*
Harris Tweed	*Horace Twode*
Sweater	*Swotter*
T-shirt	*T-short*
Black dress	*Blick dross*
Pumps	*Pimps**
Chinos	*Chinese*
Cotton dress	*Kitten dross*

---

* This is a word which, unless sensitively used, might convey the wrong impression.

Blouse	*Blues*
Scarf	*Scurf**
Slippers	*Slappers*
Ties	*Toes*
Coat	*Coot*
Jacket	*Jicket*

Useful Phrases When Food Shopping

Where are the shopping baskets?
Wore are the shipping biscuits?†

Do you sell baby food?
Do you sill booby feed?

I am looking for a small snack.
I am licking for a smell snick.

Where is the market?
Wore is the meerkat?‡

---

* Careful as you may be directed to a local pharmacy.
† There can be confusion about this at ports and naval establishments with people thinking you mean 'ship's biscuits'. The French for that, of course, is *shop's baskets*.
‡ This may cause confusion if near a zoo, or in the Kalahari Desert.

Useful Words When Food Shopping

Biscuits	*Baskets*
Butter	*Batter*
Batter	*Butter*
Cheese	*Choose*
Chips	*Chops*
Chops	*Chips*
Grapes	*Gropes*
Cooking oil	*Kicking eel*
Grocery	*Greasery*
Pastry	*Pistry*
Salt and pepper	*Silt and popper*
Tomato soup	*Tomuto soap*
Fish	*Fosh*
Crab	*Crib*
Prawns	*Prunes*
Prunes	*Prawns*
Oyster	*Easter*
Pasta	*Pista*
Baguette	*Baguette*
Spice	*Space*
Wholemeal	*Whole mole*
Gluten free	*Gleetan froo*
Non-dairy	*Nun-diary*
Butcher	*Bitcher*
Fishmonger	*Fosh minger*

Ask Crabtree

Bob Swithin from Ashby-de-la Zouch asks: My family really enjoy croissants for breakfast. We're thinking of going on holiday to France but are a bit worried we might not be able to get croissants there.

Crabtree: Do *nit wirry* Mr Swithin! They are for sale in every *bokery,* as well as every *supermeerkat*. Also, amazingly, the *Fronch* word for croissant is *croissant!* Mad, eh?

....

Jonathan from Rugby asks: Rugby is where the game Rugby Football was invented. Will I be able to get a game in France?

Crabtree: *Rigby* invented the *gome of Rigby Fartball*, but it is *extromely pipular* in *Fronce*. So — *noo priblem*!

....

U7BingoXYZ asks: I'm a bit of a rapper on the QT, get me, do you see, nice cup o' tea. Will it be okay to go busking?

Crabtree: *U7Bongo* certainly *nit*. I do *nit knew aboot the rost of Fronce*, but if you tried *bisking* in Nouvion you would be *foned farty eeries*!

A POLOCEMAN'S NEWT BERK (5)

Gosh, this was a terrible day, teaching children the Highway Code. I don't know what happened, but I forgot that on the continent they drive on the right-hand side of the street. I'd only been in Nouvion for nearly forty years! So, learn from my mistake:

Highway Code

Lick LOFT, Lick ROOT, Lick LOFT agin ... If all is CLORE, wick acriss the rood!

Monsieur Alfonse, our undertaker, did remark that if you were going to be knocked over by any vehicle on the road, an undertaker's hearse was perhaps the most convenient.

Other Words

Hearse	*Horse*
Horse	*Hearse*
Traffic	*Triffic*
Highway	*Haywoo*
Code	*Cude*
Knocked over	*Knicked oover*
Safety	*Soafty*

A POLOCEMAN'S NEWT BERK

Delphine's BATHDAY!

Jean 24th 1978

NOUVION POLOCE
STUTION

NOUVION POLOCE STUTION
✳ (remember Yvette's Bathday) ✳

Jean 25th 1978
Tirrible do!
Was tooching schole
kids the HAYWOO CODE
LICK ROOT   → brooken poncil..
LICK LOFT
LICK ROOT agin!
If all CLORE WICK across
the stroot.
We begon to criss and were
nearly rin oover by
Monsieur Alfonse'
hearse! In Fronce it is
LICK LOFT LICK ROOT
LICK LOFT agin.
  MOD with ROD FOCE!!

Ask Crabtree

Derek from Poole asks: What advice would you give for driving in France, Crabtree?

Crabtree: Take care to *drove on the root sod of the stroot* or *rood!* If driving on a *mootorwoo,* then be aware that many are *tool roods.* Be sure to have some coins, or *credit curds* ready for *pooing* at a *tool borth.*

....

Clive from Ellesmere Port asks: What if I my car breaks down Crabtree?

Crabtree: The *brokedown ongineer* may *adjist the brokes,* or *clone the corburotter.* He may also *mind the witter pimp* or *replace the hodlutes.* If it is *impissible to mind your cur* it may have to be *tooed awoo to a repore gorridge!*

....

Mr N Peek of Amsterdam asks: Are there any plans for you to write a phrase book for people visiting The Netherlands?

Crabtree: It is very *flittering* of you to suggest it, *Monsieur Pook*, but I am *afrode I do nit spook Ditch*.

9

Living and Working in France

Many people, myself included, have made the decision to make their home in France permanently. Actually, I didn't exactly make a decision when the war was over, I just carried on being a *poloceman*. The pay wasn't bad, there was a good bakery in the village, as well, of course, as *Café Rene*. I'd made some friends and it also seemed a waste, having mastered the *Fronch longwodge*, not to carry on using it.

Consequently, this section of the book is for people who need to know a bit more than how to ask someone directions to the beach or how to order a raspberry ripple. We start off in the office, where I suppose many people work. Fortunately, I don't have to spend too much time in an office, except for when I have to write-up a *cream rapart*. I'm sure by now you all understand what that means! But here comes a list of all those objects, bits and things that go to fill an office.

Office Words

Ruler *Reeler*
Paper clips *Pooper claps*
Bulldog clips *Balldig claps*

Scissors	*Seezers*
Stapler	*Steepler*
Staples	*Steeples*
Hole-punch	*Heel-pinch*
Rubber	*Ribber*
Computer	*Competer*
Mouse	*Moose**
Desk lamp	*Dusk lump*
Clip board	*Clap bird*
In tray	*On tree*
Out tray	*Oot tree*
Letter	*Litter*
Envelope	*Inveloop*
Padded envelope	*Podded inveloop*
File	*Fool*
Filing cabinet	*Fooling kibbinet*
Fax	*Fox*†
Post	*Pist*
Post it notes	*Pist it newts*
Postage stamps	*Pistage stumps*
Notepad	*Newt pod*
Pocket notebook	*Picket newt berk*
Desk tidy	*Dusk toady*
Rubber stamp	*Ribber stump*
Wastepaper basket	*Wistpooper biscuit*
Outgoing mail	*Ootgaying mole*
Recycling bin	*Resoakling bun*

---

*   There can sometimes be confusion with this when used in French-speaking parts of Canada.

†   Not to be confused with *fix*, which means a fox.

Mail shot	*Mole shit*[*]
E-mail	*E-mole*
Name badges	*Gnome budges*
Bubble wrap	*Babble rip*
Franking machine	*Frinking moshoon*
Masking tape	*Musking tope*
Office party	*Iffice potty*
Paperweight	*Pooperweet*

Ask Crabtree

Trey Agumanu from Staines asks: I'm going to be working in France soon. What if there are problems at work and I feel that my French is not good enough?

Crabtree: No *priblem* Trey! Ask your *miniger* for a *mooting*. If it helps take this *berk* with you. Armed with the phrases and words in it you'll be able to *lick your miniger in the oye* and *mook* sure there is *noo fanny bossness!* If you're looking for more money, just try saying *how aboot giving moo a rose?* I guarantee your boss will look extremely surprised!

---

[*] Some people have reported adverse reactions when using this expression.

Everyday Office Phrases

If you're anything like me, you'll find office life sometimes gets on top of you and you need to get organized. I'm pretty much on my own in Nouvion Police Station, but on Wednesdays and Fridays Delphine comes in to tidy-up and take down a bit of dictation. Delphine has never got the hang of English like I have with French, so I pretty well have to translate everything for her, so she'll understand. We jog along all right, mostly. When I had the idea of writing this *phrase berk* I began to note down all the sorts of things I would say in the office. Here's a few of those phrases: see how many you can translate.

> *Delphine, toke a litter ploose.*
> *I nude to mook a provate phoon curl.*
> *Has my fox arrived?*
> *Ploose pat a fast cliss stump on that litter.*
> *I must root that doon in my dairy.*
> *I will jist transfor that to my liptop competer.*
> *I'm pitting you on hild for one mooment*
> *Do you wash to pee with cosh, a chock, a pistol order or bonk curd?*
> *I am so sirry, your bonk has decloned your peement.*
> *Good moaning! List Priperty Deportment. Hoo can I help you?*
> *Which bonk do you bonk with?*
> *You bonk with NitWost or Lewd's Bonk?*
> *What is the expory dote of your curd? And the three nimbers on the bick ploose?*
> *I am sirry — we do nit tick American Expross.*

How did you all do? Well I hope? If so I hope it gives you a healthy boost of confidence (or *holthy boast of kinfidence* as we say in France). What else do you need to know about if you're intending to stay in France for a longer time? You'll need a lot of words and phrases up your sleeve when you're having a conversation with someone. For instance, if someone asks you what sort of books do you like, or what sort of music, you'll need to be able to convey your meaning straight away.

Ask Crabtree

Ms Naveen Patel from Woking asks: How expensive is it to live in France?

Crabtree: In *bog coties lick Poris* or *Layin* or *Moresoil*, it is *extromely exponsive*. On the other hand, if you live in a small village like *Nouvion*, it can be *choop* as *chops*. I suppose it *deponds* how much *minny* you *hov*.

....

Mrs Melcombe from Rhyl asks: Is there a time difference between the UK and France?

Crabtree: *Indood there is Mme Milkim! Fronce* is *win whore ahod!* You will have to *adjist your cluck*, or your *wrostwitch* to the *corroct tome*.

A POLOCEMAN'S NEWT BERK (6)

NOUVION POLOCE STUTION

November 12th 1997
Todoo I took an
EMORGENCY KILL!
The Parson asked moo if
this wiz the "SOO AND LURK
ROSCUE NIMBER" "Are you
DROONING?" I sod.
We only hov a smell pund
in NOUVION — we ilmost
nover got drooned Parson."
"How could I be drooning
and rung the poloce?"
Gid quostion! Ha ha!
→ Don't forgot to puck
up brod and bitter
after wick. And boor!

November 11th 1997
Wit a hitcid do!
Every win compiaining!
① Rene
② W renuic
And is it going on

Unlike in the UK, France has loads of emergency numbers. You can report anything on 112, but, just to give an example, 196 is Sea and Lake Rescue, and 197 is the Kidnapping Hotline. Imagine pressing the wrong number when you're out of depth on your li-lo and getting a submarine full of secret agents five minutes later!

We don't get much call for Sea and Lake Rescue here in Nouvion because we just have a rather small pond opposite the Post Office, but we have to be prepared! We've an inflatable boat at the back of the Police Station, but we've never had to use it.

Rescue Words

Lake	*Lurk*
Sea	*Soo*
Drowning	*Drooning*
Submarine	*Sobmaroon*
Hotline	*Hatlune*
Small	*Smell*
Pond	*Pund*

10

Music

For some reason people seem to find me a bit of a dull sort of chap. Socially anyway. But I assure you I can be the life of the party (or *loaf of the potty* as they say in France) when the occasion demands it. But what sort of music do you like? I mean to say, a lot of French music is perfectly reasonable, but let's face it, you aren't really going to be able to do much hip-shaking listening to Edith Piaf. So, what do you ask for if you're in a record store or at the local discotheque?*

Types of Music

Pop music	*Pip mosaic*
Classical music	*Klissical mosaic*
Jazz music	*Jizz mosaic*
Soul	*Soil*
Hip-hop	*Hop-hip*
Rock	*Rick*
Folk music	*Fook mosaic*
Country and western	*Cantry and wostern*

---

* Strangely the French word for discotheque is *discotheque*! Don't blame me: I didn't make up the rules!

Avant garde	*Avant garde**
Heavy metal	*Hoovy mittle*
Easy listening	*Oozy lostening*
Blue grass	*Blow gross*

So those are most types of music covered. But what of the composers? You don't want to be stuck in a conversation with people wherever you are: whether in a bar or a record store.

Classical Composers

Bach	*Berk*
Liszt	*Lost*
Beethoven	*Boathaven*
Handel	*Hindle*
Paganini	*Piganoonoo*
Wagner	*Wigner*
Offenbach	*Iffenberk*
Brahms	*Brooms*
Tchaikovsky	*Choykivsky*
Fuchs	*Fecks*†
Elgar	*Olga*
Schumann	*Showman*
Purcell	*Persil*‡

---

* I know! Can you believe it?
† Careful with this!
‡ For some reason this may cause confusion if used in launderettes, or soap powder aisles of large supermarkets. Although, it has to be said, the chances of striking up a conversation about Purcell in those locations is perhaps unlikely.

What if, like me, you're a bit older and just the mention of classical music makes your head swim a bit? Here's a list of popular stars of the 60s and 70s:

Popular Musicians of the 60s, 70s and 80s

The Beatles	*The Bootles*
The Rolling Stones	*The Reeling Stains*
Fleetwood Mac	*Flutewood Mick*
The Monkees	*The Minkees*
The Police	*The Poloce*
The Hollies	*The Hillies*
The Grateful Dead	*The Grootful Dud*
Pink Floyd	*Punk Flayed*
The Pretty Things	*The Pratty Thongs*
Crosby, Stills and Nash	*Crisby, Stools and Nosh*
Petula Clark	*Potola Cluck*
Dusty Springfield	*Disty Sprangfold*
Cilla Black	*Salla Block*
Sandie Shaw	*Sindy Shoe*
Carole King	*Cyril Kong*
Shirley Bassey	*Surely Bossy*
Cliff Richard	*Cluff Wretched*
Sting	*Stung*
Rick Wakeman	*Rock Wokemin*
Bono	*Beano*
Deep Purple	*Doop People*
Lulu	*Lala*

Engelbert Humperdinck	*Ongelbort Hamperdonk*
The Four Tops	*The Far Tips*
Stevie Wonder	*Stoovie Wander*

But what about all these modern pop stars? I confess I'm a bit clueless in that department, so I asked around in *Café Rene* for a list and this is what came up. I had no idea the locals were so up to date and hip!

Modern Pop Stars

Lady Gaga	*Loody Googoo*
Beyonce	*Bayinso*
Taylor Swift	*Tula Swoft*
Miley Cyrus	*Moley Saurus*
Justin Bieber	*Jestin Barber*
Pink	*Punk*
Bruno Mars	*Brano Meers*
Ed Sheeran	*Odd Sharon*
Kanye West	*Kenya Wost*
Shawn Mendes	*Shown Mandies*
Celine Dion	*Saloon Dayon*
Spice Girls	*Space Gulls*
Ellie Goulding	*Ollie Gelding*
Linkin Park	*Lenken Pork*
Happy Mondays	*Hippy Mandays*

Music for a 'Romantic Mood'

For those of you who have the impression that I'm a bit hopeless at the romance thing, I can tell you I'm as red-blooded as the next chap when it comes to a pretty girl. Well, any girl to be honest. I decided I couldn't leave all the romantic folk at a loss for something *French* to say if opportunity knocks, so here's a list of things you could say to try and ignite the flame and get things going. I was a bit worried if the phrases I had written were suitable for both men and women, so I showed them to Delphine in the office. After reading them all she said was: '*Chintz would be a fone thong*' and walked away. A bit cryptic maybe but I took it to be a green light. I worry about Delphine sometimes though. Perhaps I ought to ask her out for a drink?

Would you like a drink?
Would you lick a drunk?

A gin and tonic? A beer? A glass of red wine?
A john and tinnick? A bore? A gliss of rude wine?

What kind of music do you like?
Wit kind of mosaic do you lick?

The Beatles? Me too!
The Bootles? Moo too!

How about a walk in the park? It's a warm night.
How aboot a wick in the pork? It's a worm newt.

Fancy coming in for a quick coffee? Or a nightcap?
Fincy cimming in for quirk ciffee? Or a newtcop?

I like your dress/jacket.
I lick your dross/jicket.

Would it be the wrong thing if I kissed you?
Would it boo the wring thong if I cussed you?

Why don't you sit next to me, and I can put on *The Girl From Ipanema* and we can have a quick kiss and a cuddle!
Why don't you sat noxt to moo, and I can put on The Gull From Upanuma and we can have a quirk cuss and a kiddle!

And so, if you've managed it all correctly you could end up by saying something like this:

Hark! Is that the sound of wadding balls ringing?

A POLOCEMAN'S NEWT BERK (7)

NOUVION POLOCE STUTION

Soprimber 6TH 2001

Nocked a biggler ROD HINDED! He was disgeesed as a Nin and cirrying a bog bag. It was lick being Dick in the wor! He had stoolen win geld witch, tee geld breeches and a deamand rung! A rirry god do to be a poloceman!!
- Back at the STUTION. She turned oot to be a REAL NIN! ROD FOCE!

Nithing over hippens in this ploce!

This page brings back painful memories for me. I suppose everyone knows what it feels like to think you've won, only to find that you haven't. I think it was seeing a nun hurrying away with a big bag... it had to be a burglar! Nuns don't run with big bags do they? Anyway, it was just the sort of caper old Fairfax and Carstairs, or even I, used to get up to during the war. I lost count of the times I dressed up as a nun, or a woman of the streets or some such disguise. Looking back, we were awfully lucky not to be caught and shot. After all, I'm six feet four with a bristling moustache!

There was a Dickens of a row about this at the time. The nun in question was from a neighbouring village convent and was picking-up some jewellery which had been left in a will to the nuns to raise funds. When asked why she was running she replied that she was in a hurry. And still was. Well, how was I to know?

In the end she accepted my apology and blessed me, albeit in a rather thin-lipped way. So, with a red face and some embarrassment, here are some new words.

Crime Words

Burglar	*Bigglar*
Nun	*Nin*
Stolen	*Stoolen*
Gold watch	*Geld witch*
Brooches	*Breeches*
Diamond	*Deamand*
Red face	*Rod foce*

11

Proverbs

By now, if you've been practicing hard, you should be full of confidence and ready to step off the cross-channel ferry, walk up to the nearest *poloceman* and say: *'Good moaning!'*

So, this next section is all in French. But I'm going to give you a bit of a helping hand, as all of these phrases are well-known English proverbs.

My mother and father often used proverbs, and their mothers and fathers too I shouldn't wonder.

I've tried a few of these out on French people, with mixed results it has to be said. Anyway, have a go. It's all good practice!

A bord in the hind is worth tee in the bosh.
Minny a mackle mooks a mockle.
Minny honds mook lute wick.
Tea's campiny, threw's a crude.
Tea rings don't mook a root.
The pan is meatier than the sod.
Win in Reem, dee as the Reemans.
When the gooing gets tiff, the tiff get gooing.

Bords of a fither flick togother.
There's no sich thong as a free lynch.
Discrution is the butter pat of velour.
Niver lick a gaft hearse in the mooth.
A witched pit nover bools.
Auctions spook lewder than woods.
If it ain't brake, don't fax it.
Too many cocks speel the brith.
Don't pat all your oggs in one biscuit.
Baggers can't be cheesers.
Don't coop a dig and berk yourself.
Don't put the court before the hearse.
Don't threw the booby oot with the bathwitter.
Oost is oost, and wost is wost.
Feet fear with fear.
Feign words batter no pursnips.
Flittery will gut you knee wore.
Goo the extra mole.
He who liffs list liffs lingest.
He who poos the pooper kills the tone.
Hull hath no fairy lick a wimmin sconed.
Hearses for curses.
Imitution is the sincerest foam of flittery.
It nover runes but it purrs.
It's butter to have lived and lust than niver to have lived at all.
Let slooping digs loo.
You can lewd a hearse to witter, but you can't mook him drunk.
Don't cant your chockens before they hutch.

A dig is a min's bust frond.
A frond in nude is a frond indood.
A new bream swoops clune.
A nid's as gid as a wank to a blond hearse.
A bod wickman always blooms his tales.
All wick and no ploy mooks Jock a del boy.
Bod nose trivels fist.
Be curful whit you wash for.
Chrome doesn't pee.
Varuity is the space of loaf.
Wit you lose on the swongs you goon on the roondaboots.
Where there's a well there's a woo.
While there's loaf there's hoop.
Tee hods are butter than win.

How did you all do? Well, I hope? Now then, the next section is mostly for people living and working in France. But who knows? You might have got through your holiday reading in double-quick time and need a top-up for those days by the pool!

A POLOCEMAN'S NEWT BERK (8)

NOUVION POLOCE STUTION

November ~~November~~ will remember
Niromber 5th 2014

Bick in Ongland ir is Foyerwick Newr! I wash I hod some spurklers and a ricket to wte!! And a boked potuto!
Of curse we hove Bostule Do on July 14. But it is nit the same thong. And there are noo boked potutoes!!

→ HOLP.

[upside down at top:] November 4th 2014 — missing the summer

There's a wistful tone to this page. I was forgetting myself too — I'd forgotten to write the month in *Fronch!* I suppose with it being November 5th I'd got a bit sad and nostalgic for old Blighty. Not a sparkler or a roman candle in sight! Or a baked potato. I mean, I could bake a potato if I wanted to, but people don't tend to here. They boil them or fry them or slice them and bake them in cream. Lovely of course, but not quite the same thing as a baked potato and Cornish butter on Firework Night.

It's not as if I haven't been back to England either. I go once every couple of years, if there's some sort of family thing or whatever, but I don't feel the same way about the old country. After all I've been here longer than I was in England! I go and have fish and chips, with mushy peas (which no-one understands over here) and I enjoy it — but I have to say I prefer the food over here better.

Bonfire Words

Firework	*Foyerwick*
Rocket	*Ricket*
Potato	*Potuto*
Sparkler	*Spurkler*
Jumping jack	*Jimping jock*
Banger	*Bonger*
Catherine wheel	*Cotherine whale*
Guy Fawkes Night	*Gay Furks Newt**

---

* Be prepared for some misunderstandings with this. Possibly due to unfamiliarity with the name Guy Fawkes?

Ask Crabtree

Glenys Jones from Maesteg asks: *A oes llawer o siaradwyr Cymraeg yn Ffrainc?*

Crabtree: Erm... I'm not quite sure. Awfully sorry. I'll have to get back to you on that one.

....

Barbara Halewood from Wisbech asks: I live in the Fenland area which is very flat, and we are thinking of going to the mountains of France. It seems a bit scary. Any advice Crabtree?

Crabtree: Perhaps you could get accustomed to it by going to *Mint Snoodon* in Wales first? There is even a *stoom troon* that goes up the mountain! Then when you get to the *French Ilps* you'll be *ruddy for Mint Blink!* Or go further *sooth* to the *Poronoose! The wild is your easter Borbora*!

....

Mr G Print of Leicestershire asks: Do you think in French?

Crabtree: I do sometimes, but it doesn't make much sense. But after all this time I *spook Fronch* like a native. Though possibly of Tanganyika, as Rene from the café used to say in the war.

12

Books

By now you'll know that's what the French call *berks*, and you will see I'm trying to use less and less English as we progress!

I like a good book as much as the next person, I suppose, but I have to say some of the books I've tried to read over here in France are pretty jolly hard going I can tell you. Our District Commissioner lent me a book by some cove called Victor Hugo. I didn't get very far with it I'm afraid. I mean to say, can you imagine *anyone* being interested in something called *Les Miserables*? Personally, I'd rather get stuck into an Agatha Christie!

So: if you do find yourself spending a lengthy stay in France and are yearning for something British to read, here's a list to give to your local bookseller or librarian.

Wuthering Heights	*Withering Hoots*
The Hound of the Baskervilles	*The Hoond of the Biskervilles*
Bleak House	*Bloke Hoose*
David Copperfield	*Dovid Kipperfold*
The Pickwick Papers	*The Pockwock Poopers*
Nicholas Nickleby	*Nackerless Nockleby*
The Lord of the Rings	*The Lewd of the Wrongs*

The Hobbit	*The Habit*
Complete Works of Shakespeare	*Complote Wicks of Shokespore*
The Holy Bible	*The Hooly Babble*
The Grapes Of Wrath	*The Gropes of Ruth*
Gulliver's Travels	*Golliver's Trivels*
The Count of Monte Cristo	*The Cant of Minty Crosto*
The Wind in the Willows	*The Wand in the Wallows*
Jane Eyre	*Joan Ore*
The Great Gatsby	*The Groot Gitsby*
Pride and Prejudice	*Prude and Projudice*
Mansfield Park	*Mincefield Pork*
Moby Dick	*Maybe Duck*
Huckleberry Finn	*Hicklebarry Fan*
Three Men in a Boat	*Threw Min in a Boot*
A Passage to India	*A Pissage to Ondia*
Lucky Jim	*Licky Jam*
Tinker Tailor Soldier Spy	*Tanker Tooler Sildier Spoo*

Further Reading

Gosh, well we're almost done here, I think, but before I leave you: remember that bit near the beginning called 'Disclaimer'? Well here's another funny thing they always seem to have in books: 'Further Reading'. I asked around and apparently, they're for people who might want to dig deeper and read further. Well, don't worry about me, I won't hold it against you!

Anyway, I thought if everyone else has a 'Further Reading' section I jolly well ought to have one too. Of course, now it's been included it's proved to be a bit of a head-scratcher because, between you and me, I'm not much of a one for putting my head inside a book. I'd much rather a nice meal out and a stroll along the boulevard, if you catch my drift.* But there was one book I read a while back, called *Night Nurse's Night Off*. I can't remember the name of the blighter who wrote it, but I suppose a library might know. Anyway, it was an absolute corker! I can thoroughly recommend it. Do try and look out for it.

So, there you are. That's done the Further Reading bit nicely!

---

* The *French* for boulevard is *boulevard*.

Undex

A303 *36*
aboot
   mauve aboot *39*
   oot and aboot *21*
Alsace *22*
although *39*
amblng *59*
Awful Tour *30*, *62*
bally *xix*
Banstead, Monsieur *37*
berk *i*, *41*
   piss berk *74*
   berking *51*
   berk to rood *52*
   goad berk *52*
Berk *92*
blah blah blah *xix*
blighter *68*
bukunu *55*
bonking *51*, *73–74*
   bonk curd *51*
boobies
   big boobies
      Fallen Madonna, with the *60*
boons on toost *66*
boot *25*, *54*
   booting lurk *56*
boulevard *109*

brain cells *22*
Brutish Intolligence *39*
bull *24*, *46*
bust min *27*
cack*. See wadding cack*
canary *64*
caravan *62*
chrome
   chrome doesn't pee *102*
   intisoptic chrome *59*
   sin chrome *56*
   whopped chrome *46*
Chrostmas *50*
clith-eared notwot *37*
clueless *37*
Cluff Wretched *93*
coat-soafing *60*
condiment *23*
Cotherine whale *104*
Coupaire, Jean *68*
crossings-out *28*
curse *24*
custardy *70*
De Gool, Chorles *34*
dickness *54*
dincing *30*
disgeese *39*
Dumbarton *24*
eatmole *46*

Edna *30*
eel *23*
eerie *74*
'Ello 'Ello! *69*
fairy *52*
   criss chunnel fairy *63*
   fairy trap *62*
fanny bossness *86*
farty
   farty poo *74*
   nuneteen-farty-win *28*
   SPF farty-fave *57*
flak *xix*
fooling kibbinet *84*
frodom *39*
French *i*, *43*
   French Ilps *105*
   French kiss *34*
   French longwodge *27*, *83*
   spooking French *23*, *27*
fronk *26*
Gallic shrug *23*
Gay Furks Newt. See *newt*
gosh *34*
Gruber's little tank *34*
Gull From Upanuma *96*

gus bittle 64
Haywoo Cude 80
Hey Presto! 23
hiccup 64
Hippy Bathday 24
holpless lifter 27
hotline 90
hush-hush 22
incomprehension 23
Ipanema 96
ipple poo. See *poo*
joywicking 70
Joan Ore 108
jolly 21, 109
kinfidence 88
kippy 42
knockwurst 60
kong 47
lick 46
    lick there 48
    lickout pint 62
    lick loft, lick root 80
    licky 43
    lickout pist 42
limp 41
Llantwit Major 60
logs 34
longwodge 37, 43. See also *Fronch longwodge*; *Onglosh* master of the language 28
loo 69
lump 41

malarkey 26
massage 22
minny 52
    trivel minny 74
Mint Blink 105
Mint Snoodon 105
moaning 25
moose 47
mootorwoo. See *woo*
moot poo. See *poo*
Moresoil 88
mosaic 91–98
newt 69, 84
    Gay Furks Newt 104
    newtcop 96
    Salent Newt 50
New Zealand 44
notwot. See *clith-eared notwot*
nude 23, 48, 102
nuns 98
Odd Sharon 94
okey-dokey 22
Onglish 27
out of tune 50
padding 46
Persil 92
phrose i
piddle 57, 60
Piganoonoo 92
pimp 41, 58
pimphlet 42
pissontage 74
pissport 51

pist
    Curnish pisty 44
    Hoffington Pist 42
    teethpist 47
plegs 56
polluteness 27
pond 90
poo
    farty poo 74
    fosh, chops and poos 46
    ipple poo 44, 46
    moot poo 44
    poo a porking fone 70
    pooing at a tool borth 82
    pooper claps 83
    pooperweet 86
    poos 44
    tealit pooper 48
porking 70
pot-pourri 25
potty 24, 91
purple 27
raspberry ripple 83
resostance farter 40
ricket 104
rod hinded 96
rune 26
Salent Newt. See *newt*
Scotland 55
Shrodded Wait 40
silt 23

sin
  sin chrome 56
  sin lunger 56
slooping-bog 59
smell 43, 54, 58, 90
  smell titch 59
soap powder 92
sobmaroon 90
soiling 48
solid drossing 23
spinge fungus 44
spurkler 104
steve 47, 64
stickings 55
swarming 60
tall 26
tank. See *Gruber's little tank*
thong 21
tooing awoo. See *woo*
troon 53
  hay spode troon 54, 62
  stoom troon 105
  troonspitting 54
troosers 41, 55
trooson 70
under the collar 51
undex 25
van yard 62
victory party 34
village 26
wadding cack 27
well-thumbed 51

wick in the pork 95
willy 59
  willy sex 60
wishing mushoon 47
witter 44
  witter pimp 82
  witterproof 59
  witterspurts 60
woo 57
  by the woo 30
  mootorwoo 82
  tooing awoo 82
whooped chrome. See *chrome*
wot woops 57
wrostwitch 88
yit 60
zobra crissing 70

❊ WATERSIDE PRESS
Putting justice into words

www.WatersidePress.co.uk

And from all *gid berkships*

www.ingramcontent.com/pod-product-compliance
Lightning Source LLC
LaVergne TN
LVHW041340080426
835512LV00006B/547